The American Millennial Attraction to Socialism:

Comparing the Economies of Chinese Communism, Crony Corporate Capitalism, European Crony Socialism, and the American Free Enterprise Entrepreneurial Economy.

Laurie Thomas Vass

The Great American Business & Economics Press
GABBY Press

Printed in the United States of America
May 2020

ISBN 978-1-5136-6085-1

ISBN: 978-1-5136-6085-1

9 781513 660851

Bulk orders of 10 or more books eligible for 35% discount.
Gabbypress.com

The American Millennial Attraction to Socialism

Table of Contents

Introduction. The American Millennial Attraction to Socialism.

Our book extends the analysis of the Annual Report on US Attitudes Toward Socialism to explain why so many young Americans are attracted to socialism.

We describe a much more fair and just economic system than socialism for the millennials to support.

Our book compares the four major economic models in the world in order to help millennials better understand their possible choices about the best economic system, judged from their own perspective of fairness and social justice.

Our book addresses the topics of:
The American Millennial Attraction to Socialism.
The Chinese Communist Crony Economy.
The Crony Corporate Capitalist Economy.
The European Crony Socialist Economy.
The American Free Enterprise Entrepreneurial Economy.
Envisioning A New American Knowledge Creation Innovation Economy.
Buchanan's Fair Constitutional Rules as the Foundation of the Entrepreneurial Economy.

We argue that Chinese communism, European socialism, and American crony capitalism, are all variants of crony capitalism that attempt to use government to distribute financial benefits to politically connected agents.

The key common characteristic of the three crony collectivist economies is profit exploitation by the elites over the production value produced by the non-elites.

Cronyism exploitation replaces the Marxist concept of capitalist exploitation of the workers with crony exploitation of non-elites.

The set of cronies who benefit from cronyism attempt to maximize a group collectivist concept, which is commonly described as a social welfare function.

In their case, their selfish social welfare function acts as a substitute for individualist national welfare function.

In the 3 collectivist economies, the entire society is seen as a synthetic entity, whose national welfare is measured by aggregate social indicators like GDP, fairness and income equality.

The propaganda of the collectivist society is that the elites know better than common citizens what promotes social welfare, and must, therefore, have the unchecked political power to exploit the production value of the non-elites in order to obtain the tax revenue to achieve better social welfare outcomes in fairness and income equality.

In contrast to group social welfare, we argue that only one economic system attempts to maximize individual welfare, which we call the American Free Enterprise Entrepreneurial Economy.

In the individualist innovation economy, social welfare is judged by aggregating all individual welfare functions into a national social welfare function.

Individuals are free to maximize their own welfare, and have property rights to enjoy the profits that they create through their own individual initiative.

We argue that young Americans do not know the difference between group social welfare functions and individualist welfare functions, and do not know how to evaluate the fair outcomes between a collectivist economy and an individualist economy.

In the collectivist societies, the concept of fairness is judged by political elites who determine fair outcomes, after income has been earned.

In the individualist societies, fairness constitutes the ability of the individual to appropriate the income that they produce.

Millennials are attracted to socialism because they believe that the socialist economic systems are more fair than their concept of American capitalism, which is the crony corporate capitalist version of capitalism.

Most young people in America do not know the difference between Milton Friedman and Lord Keynes, and end up in the economic muddle of Milton Keynes, embracing a fairy tale socialism that is antithetical to their desired state of fairness and social justice.

We explain that innovation economics is the most fair system, and that if millennials understood how the free enterprise entrepreneurial economy worked, that they would switch their allegiance from socialism to innovation economics.

We conclude that the progress towards a fair American entrepreneurial economy can be improved by visualizing the entire economy as a knowledge creation enterprise, modeled upon the logic of a regional metro block chain, whose end goal is the commercialization of radical new technology, and the creation of new future markets.

Chapter 1. The American Millennial Attraction to Socialism.

In the recent Annual Report on US Attitudes Toward Socialism, (Victims of Communism Memorial Foundation, YouGov, 2019.), communism is viewed favorably by 33% of American millennials, an increase in favorability of 8% from 2018.

At least 70% of millennials would be somewhat likely to vote for a socialist candidate, and 20% said they would be "extremely likely" to vote for a socialist candidate.

A majority of millennials reported that communism was presented more favorably than capitalism in elementary and middle school.

About 37% of millennials think America is one of the most unequal societies in the world.

More than half of American millennials think the highest earners are not paying their fair share of taxes, and 47% say a complete change of our economic system is needed, including 20% who say that American society would be better off if all private property were abolished.

Millennials conflate and confuse the terms "fairness," with democracy. For young people, democracy is not defined by voting, it is defined by obtaining fair democratic outcomes in income distribution.

In their reality, democracy is redefined as democratic equality, and has nothing to do with citizen political participation or government by the consent of the governed.

Millennials have been taught that the entire dynamic of economic history is the exploitation of workers by the capitalist class.

Social justice, for millennials, means that something of value is unfairly taken away from the disadvantaged groups. Democracy, as fairness, means that the socialist government would appropriate the profits, and redistribute the unearned capitalist profits to more deserving poor people.

The concept the millennials are getting at with "democracy as fairness," is to correct the unfairness of crony capitalism.

Freedom Works, explains the relationship between fairness and crony capitalism, in their work, titled, Fundamentals of Free Enterprise.

They write,

"The issue at hand today is that crony capitalists work with corrupt politicians in order to unfairly line their pockets.... capitalism can lead to "crony capitalism," where businessmen are in bed with the government."

A 2014 Reason-Rupe survey asked respondents to use their own words to describe socialism and found millennials who viewed it favorably were more likely to think of it as people being kind or "being together."

Emily Ekins and Joy Pullmann, in their article, Millennials Don't Know What Socialism Is, (February 15, 2016), wrote,

"The (millennial) concept of socialism stems from the idea that everyone, regardless of his or her achievements and efforts, should be rewarded equally or at least rewarded according to his or her needs—"From each according to his ability, to each according to his needs" as Karl Marx popularized."

Sean Vazquez, a writer for HuffPost, in his article, "This Is Why Millennials Favor Socialism," (April 13, 2017), also emphasized the millennial concept of "democracy as fairness."

He writes,

"Millennials are re-defining the word socialism, equating it with a "gentler" way of life, while maintaining the American value of working hard to get ahead. Taking care of each other, while enjoying the life we've been given…Fewer job opportunities limit the upward mobility of Millennials. The American Dream seems to be out of reach for those just entering the labor market."

The millennials believe that the function of government in the socialist rule of law is to restore the "value" that was "unjustly" taken away from labor.

In order to restore the value taken from workers, the end state of equal income means that everyone starts the economic competition as equals, at their birth.

In other words, the desired end state of fairness, for millennials, looks like the social equality of Chinese communism, where citizens begin the economic race, and end the economic race, exactly where they started.

Chapter 2. The Chinese Communist Economy.

The Chinese economy can be characterized as a top-down political system of state-controlled, imperial crony capitalism.

There are two parts to the state capitalism. One part is the set of state-owned corporations, and the other part are quasi-private corporations, located in the provinces, that are more market based in terms of prices and competition.

In the state-owned enterprises, there is no distinction between the state and the enterprise. All profits generated by the enterprise immediately belong to the state, which makes all income distribution and investment allocation decisions.

The state owned firms are called "National Champions" and they are very profitable.

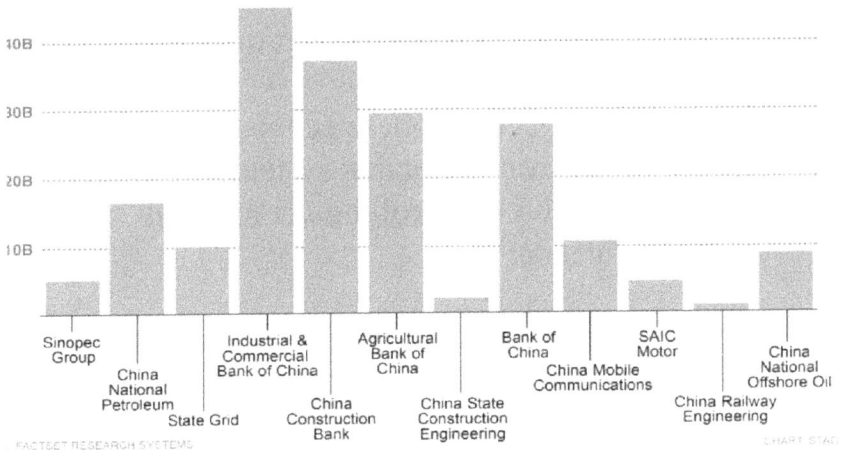

In the quasi-private firms, at the regional level, the firms compete for profits, based upon a market price system.

Profits are taxed and flow from the regional level to the centralized Communist Party.

The value of competition at the regional firm level for the CCP is that the market prices act as shadow prices for the central government in setting the value of production in state-owned enterprises.

In addition to setting shadow prices, the regional firms act to promote technological innovation, directed by the central government.

The smaller regional firms allow the central government to experiment with new technology to determine which firms are more profitable.

In most respects, the Chinese economy functions much like the crony capitalist system in America, with political elites controlling the national economic agenda.

The Communist Party maintains command over the economy by having top party officials or family members control state-owned several key industries.

For example, Jiang Mianheng, the son of former Party leader Jiang Zemin, is known as China's "Telecommunications King" due to his sizable interests and control over the communications industry.

As was noted by Minxin Pei in "China's Crony Capitalism: The Dynamics of Regime Decay," (2016),

"By forming dense networks of connections (guanxi) with private businessmen, officials can generate lucrative profits by, as Xi Jinping, the general secretary of the Chinese Communist Party, points out, turning the public authority entrusted to them into instruments to seek private gains."

Pei notes that the Chinese crony capitalism economy allows Chinese politicians to allocate profits towards family members and cronies, which results in high amounts of bribery and corruption.

In their article, State Capitalism vs. Private Enterprise, Chen, et.al. note how the regional firms are controlled, through credit allocation, by the central bank in Beijing. (Donghua Chen, Dequan Jiang, Alexander Ljungqvist, Haitian Lu, & Mingming Zhou, Research Briefs in Economic Policy No. 28, June 17, 2015, Available at SSRN).

They note the perverse outcomes in the dynamics between the regional firms, that attempt to allocate profits to profitable opportunities, and the state-owned enterprises that allocate profits to their friends and families.

"Private enterprises in China are often credit-rationed by state banks and face higher interest rates. State groups, by contrast, reallocate capital from good investment opportunity to poor-investment-opportunity member firms."

The corporate leaders of the state corporations seek to maximize their own financial welfare, consistent with the theory explained by James Buchanan, in the American context of crony capitalism. (The Reason of Rules: Constitutional Political Economy, Brennan, Geoffrey and Buchanan, James M., Cambridge University Press, 2008.).

According to Chen, et.al.,

> "State group chairmen appear to let their career incentives influence their internal capital allocation decisions. Not only do we find that internal capital allocations are used to prop up large and struggling employers with poor prospects, consistent with the policy aims of the CCP. We also find that capital allocations are particularly distorted when group chairmen are up for promotion and cease to be distorted once a group chairman becomes ineligible for promotion under the CCP's rules on mandatory retirement...Indeed, the very purpose of Chinese state capitalism is to entrench ruling elites, not liberate oppressed masses."

As described in Diagram 1, at the top of the system is the Chinese Communist Party (CCP). The profits from the bottom of the economic system flow to the top of the system.

Diagram 1.

China Central Government CCP and Local/Provincial Government

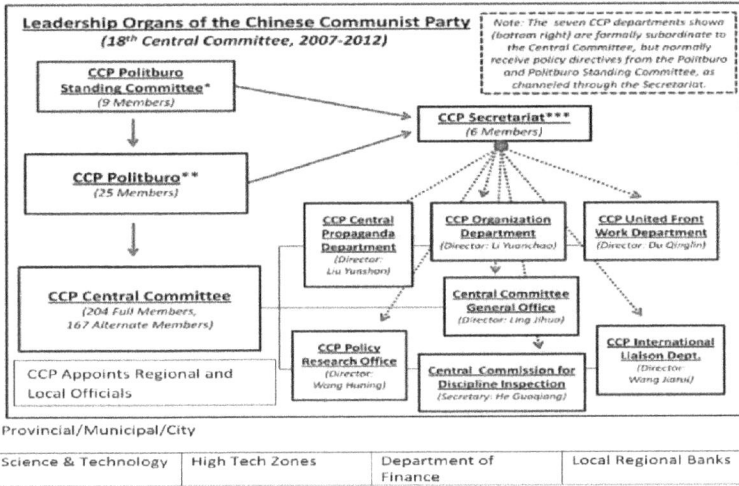

Leadership Organs of the Chinese Communist Party (18th Central Committee, 2007-2012)	Note: The seven CCP departments shown (bottom right) are formally subordinate to the Central Committee, but normally receive policy directives from the Politburo and Politburo Standing Committee, as channeled through the Secretariat.

CCP Politburo Standing Committee* (9 Members)

CCP Secretariat* (6 Members)

CCP Politburo (25 Members)

CCP Central Propaganda Department (Director: Liu Yunshan)

CCP Organization Department (Director: Li Yuanchao)

CCP United Front Work Department (Director: Du Qinglin)

CCP Central Committee (204 Full Members, 167 Alternate Members)

Central Committee General Office (Director: Ling Jihua)

CCP Policy Research Office (Director: Wang Huning)

CCP International Liaison Dept. (Director: Wang Jiarui)

CCP Appoints Regional and Local Officials

Central Commission for Discipline Inspection (Secretary: He Guoqiang)

Provincial/Municipal/City

Science & Technology	High Tech Zones	Department of Finance	Local Regional Banks

The CCP convenes its National Party Congress (NPC) every five years to set major policies and choose the Central Committee, which comprises around 370 members and alternates including ministers, senior regulatory officials, provincial leaders, and military officers.

The Central Committee acts as a sort of board of directors for the CCP, and its mandate is to select the Politburo, which has twenty-five members.

All of the 370 members of the Central Committee are also members of the Communist Party, and all of them are cronies, engaged in state-level corruption.

In turn, the Politburo elects through backroom negotiations the Politburo Standing Committee, which functions as the epicenter of the CCP's power and leadership.

The governors of China's provinces and autonomous regions and mayors of its centrally controlled municipalities are appointed by the CCP, in Beijing, after receiving the nominal consent of the National People's Congress (NPC).

Part of the dysfunction of the Chinese crony capitalist economy is that powerful elites, who control profit exploitation, also control the issuance of bonds and bank loans, leading to uncontrolled debt accumulation, in the state-owned enterprises.

China's central bank is called the People's Bank of China, or PBOC. The People's Bank sets currency exchange rates, interest rates, manages the supply of money, and controls the issuance of debt.

According to a recent McKinsey report, the level of gross debt in China, in 2014, was 282 percent of GDP. This includes government debt (55 percent of GDP, similar to the IMF's estimate),and debt owed by financial institutions (65 percent of GDP), nonfinancial corporations (125 percent of GDP), and households (38 percent of GDP). More recent estimates suggest that corporate debt may have risen above 150 percent of GDP by early 2016.

Because the issuance of debt is based upon crony capitalism, and is not subject to market discipline or market interest rates, most of the debt that is issued on behalf of state owned enterprises, is guided by political influence.

The rural enterprises do not obtain the same level of political preference in loans as the SOEs, and thus seek loans from foreign banks.

The access to foreign loans by the regional firms acts as a surrogate for efficient banking institutions at the central government level.

For example, in the case of Lenovo, the microeconomic development of the firm was critically contingent on the presence and operations of conventionally-efficient financial and legal institutions in Hong Kong.

In their research, A Model of China's State Capitalism, Li, et al., describe the profit exploitation dynamics of the banking system between SOEs and regional firms, like Lenovo.

They state,

> "We show how the upstream SOEs extract rents from the liberalized downstream sectors in the process of industrialization and globalization. It implies that the unusual prosperity of SOEs in China can be merely a growth-undermining symptom of the incompleteness of market-oriented reforms rather than a proof of their efficiency dominance over non-SOEs...In other words, the key upstream sectors are still largely controlled by the state, whereas the downstream industries operate under capitalism." (Li, Xi and Liu, Xuewen and Wang, Yong, A Model of China's State Capitalism, August 2015. Available at SSRN).

They conclude with their prediction of economic consequences of profit exploitation by the SOEs,

> "China's downstream private industries will be strangled by the upstream SOE monopoly and will lose international competitiveness if upstream SOEs fail to lower markups and improve productivity."

Deepak Lal, in his June 14, 2013, article, China's Statist Turn: Creating China Inc., highlighted the crony capitalist elements of this vertical profit exploitation system.
He noted,

> "The complex system marshals the massive savings of thrifty Chinese households to purposes determined by the interests of the "princelings" who increasingly control the party. Mr Godement notes that "there are many indications that China's 'princelings' (the children of past leaders) have formed a quasi-union.""

The primary objective of the CCP is to maintain totalitarian control over the population to sustain the elite privileges obtained from their crony capitalist system.

In State Capitalism vs. Private Enterprise, Chen, et.al., explain the major motivating factor of the Chinese elites in controlling profits.

> "We find evidence of the CCP's desire to avoid social unrest, both in the formal criteria by which the party judges the performance of SOE managers and in their actual

implementation: consistent with a desire to maintain socio-political stability, we show that the chairmen of state groups in our sample are rewarded with promotions for avoiding large scale job losses, which is easily the most economically important determinant of their career outcomes in our tests. Moreover, our tests show that state group chairmen are quite responsive to the career incentives the CCP gives them."

The elites use revenues from profit exploitation to maintain political control over the common citizens.

As they state,

> "We trace capital allocation decisions to the objectives of the Chinese Communist Party, which incentivizes managers to maintain social stability...capital allocations are used to prop up struggling employers in high-unemployment areas." (Chen, Donghua and Jiang, Dequan and Ljungqvist, Alexander and Lu, Haitian and Zhou, Mingming, State Capitalism vs. Private Enterprise February 6, 2017. Available at SSRN).

It would be a mistake to assume that the upward flow of profits from the regional corporations to the CCP is the only source of revenue for the CCP.

In addition to corporate profits, the CCP heavily exploits the wages of Chinese workers, based upon the communist ideology that individuals are expected to act in the interest of the Communist Party and the majority of society.

In China, minimum wage refers to the minimum monthly wage in the provinces.

The CCP does not set on minimum wage for the entire nation. Instead, each province, city or the other local administrative units set their own minimum wage according to its local economic conditions.

The minimum wage is divided into two kinds: monthly minimum wage applies to full-time workers and hourly minimum wage applies to part-time workers.

The monthly minimum wage ranges from a high of $350 month to an average low of around $200 per month.

The minimum wage is subject to a 45% personal income tax rate. The tax revenue flow upward from the regions to the CCP. Around 80 percent of urban wage earners are not subject to the individual income tax because of the high basic personal allowance.

In addition to collecting corporate profits and taxing wage income, the CCP collects a third form of revenue in the form of a value added tax on semi-finished goods in the corporate supply chains.

The system of Chinese minimum wages for production workers creates an irresistible attraction for American corporations to move production from America to China.

The dynamics of collaboration between U.S. corporations and China is the primary economic reason why the CCP is able to function on a global economic scale.

In other words, the Chinese economy could not function without the support and collaboration of U. S. crony corporations, beginning around 1999.

The U. S. corporations obtain an 80% cost saving in the hourly wages in China, to produce an equivalent production good in America.

As will be explained in the next section on American crony corporate capitalism, the global dynamic in trade with China permanently damages the American economic structure, and the financial welfare of American workers, leading to what many economists have called "a race to the bottom."

When President Trump rails against the "unfair trade deals with China," he is very careful not to identify the political actors in America responsible for implementing the NAFTA trade deals, in 1992, or the China entrance to the World Trade Organization, in 2001.

The most powerful political force in implementing and maintaining the status quo of the China unfair trade deals are the 200 member companies of the US-China Business Council.

The USCBC is a private, nonpartisan, nonprofit organization of approximately 200 American companies that do business with China.

As they modestly state on their website, the mission of the USCBC is to "Help Shape the World's Most Important Relationship."

One way the U. S. member companies helped shape the relationship, in 2001, was to designate China as a nonmarket economy when China entered the World Trade Organization.

The nonmarket status is equivalent to being an underdeveloped nation, and that status allowed the CCP to obtain favorable terms and conditions in negotiating the trade deals with the U. S., including the seven Chinese sins identified by Peter Navarro as:

- Stealing intellectual property,
- Forcing technology transfers,
- Hacking U. S. computers,
- Dumping cheap products into U. S. markets,
- Subsiding state-owned enterprises,
- Importing illegal drugs into America, including fentanyl,
- Manipulating the Chinese currency to obtain price advantages over U. S. producers.

The trade deals were promoted, by the USCBC, to U. S. citizens, and implemented in the U. S. political system, as a way of bringing China more towards international standards of open trade and civil rights.

The logic of the USCBC argument was, "No, really, the Chinese are just like you and me, and they will respond favorably to increased trade with America."

Since 2013, the unfair trade deals have had the exact opposite effect on China, leading President Xi Jinping to increase military repression and strengthen the role of SOEs.

The unfair trade deals with China explains the primary reason why China is compelled to steal American technology.

China's crony totalitarian collectivist economy is incapable of generating radical technological innovation because the entrepreneurs are prohibited from obtaining the value of their technology innovations.

On the other hand, their militaristic economy excels at reverse engineering, when they are able to steal important technology from American companies.

And, as we explain in the next section on American Crony Capitalism, stealing American technology is just fine with large global crony corporations of the USCBC, who benefit from the slave labor of trading with China.

The trade with China permanently damages technological innovation in America, which is one result of how the American Crony Capitalist Corporate Economy permanently damages the entire macro economic structure of the American economy.

The 70% of the American millennials who state they would vote for a socialist economy are embracing this Chinese militaristic, repressive society, for themselves, and for other American citizens.

Chapter 3. The American Crony Capitalist Corporate Economy.

Much of the academic analysis of American crony corporate capitalist economy addresses the micro economic effect on how individual firms use political influence to skew financial benefits to themselves.

The more damaging economic effect of crony capitalism is on the functioning of the national macro economy that has resulted in a bifurcated economic structure, comprised of large global firms who promote and benefit from global trade, and smaller regional firms located in 350 metro regions, who are not economically integrated into the globalist networks.

Paul Aligica and Vlad Tarko describe the difference between the global macro crony capitalism and the more conventional micro economic cronyism.

They state,

> "(Micro economic cronyism) refers to insiders and businesses securing narrow tax, spending, and regulatory advantages. Cronyism is one cause of wealth inequality…Crony exchanges are based on trust, loyalty, family and long-standing social networks.

(Macro economic cronysism) refers to changes of laws at the top (Congressional) level as a result of lobbying and crony relations. The (change in laws) affects the entire industry, whereas bribery (in micro economic cronysism) tends to be firm-specific and with much smaller spillover effects on reducing competition." (Paul Aligicia and Vlad Tarko, Crony Capitalism: Rent Seeking, Institutions and Ideology, Kyklos, May, 2014).

The main macro economic cost of cronyism is that the national rate of GDP growth is permanently lower because cronyism diverts scarce resources into non-productive enterprises, which are based upon political relationships, and are not based upon market prices.

Aligicia and Tarko place both the micro economic and the macro economic cronyism into the larger framework of "rent-seeking," which is a more conventional way for academics to analyze cronyism.

They state, "Our thesis is that (macro) crony capitalism is yet another type of rent-seeking society, (macro) crony capitalism is not mere rent-seeking, it is a meta-rent-seeking mechanism for securing the rents at consistently high levels…it as a quasi-technical label meant to describe a political system rife with corruption." (Huber 2002; Haber 2002). (Paul Aligicia and Vlad Tarko, Crony Capitalism: Rent Seeking, Institutions and Ideology, Kyklos, May 2014).

As they explain, meta-rent-seeking cronyism has a dual economic effect, one a micro economic effect that benefits the financial performance of individual companies, who obtain a competitive advantage over firms that did not obtain the crony benefits, and a macro economic effect that alters economic opportunity in the entire national economy for firms and citizens not plugged into the global crony system.

By placing corporate cronyism into the welfare analytics of the opportunity costs of cronyism, they make a useful distinction between one-time dead weight opportunity costs and the ongoing diversion of resources to unproductive political pursuits of privilege.

Both types of opportunity costs of cronyism place the entire macro economy on a lower trajectory of economic growth.

They cite the diversion of $1.7 trillion in TARP and ARRA bailouts as examples of the dead weight, one time losses.

In the cases of specific companies, below, who obtained the government bailout funds, the resources that were diverted from the economy represent an opportunity cost that is permanent because those funds will never be used again in the market price-based economy, that existed in the prior period of time.

American International Group (AIG) $40 billion
    TARP
JPMorgan Chase $25 billion   TARP
Wells Fargo $25 billion   TARP
GMAC Financial Services $27.3 billionTARP
Goldman Sachs $10 billion   TARP
Morgan Stanley $10 billion   TARP
General Motors and Chrysler $18.4 billion
Science Applications International Corporation
    >$300 million   ARRA
Johnson Controls Inc.   >$300 million   ARRA
URS Operating Controls >$200 million   ARRA
Duke Energy   >$200 million   ARRA
Lockheed Martin   >$200 million   ARRA
Centerpoint Energy   >$200 million   ARRA

Sources: Bauer (2010), Kiel (2008), Recovery.gov (2012).

In contrast to a one time dead weight loss to a specific company, they provide examples of the ongoing costs of lobbying and political influence, that they claim are greater, over time, than the one time, dead weight losses.

They explain,

> "Total expenditures on lobbying the federal
> government rose by almost 25 percent from
> 2007 to 2010, to more than $3.5 billion.
> Lobbying by the finance, insurance, and real-
> estate sector alone has been over $450 million
> per year since 2008, and the industry is now
> represented by approximately 2,500
> individual registered federal lobbyists. In
> addition to increasing its lobbying activities,
> the finance, insurance, and real-estate sector
> has also increased political donations given
> directly to federal political campaigns. These
> donations are made largely through PAC
> contributions, rising from $287 million during
> the 2006 election cycle to $503 million during
> the 2008 election cycle and $319 million
> during the 2010 election cycle."

In addition to the one time dead weight losses and
the ongoing political losses, in the language of
welfare economics, the winners in crony capitalism
are never able to compensate the losers, and the
losses are permanent and irrevocable because the
structure of equal opportunities in the prior economy
have been destroyed.

In other words, as a result of the change in laws, the entire economy is on a lower trajectory of economic growth, and the lower level of economic growth causes a loss to the economy that can never be recovered.

To paraphrase Lord Keynes on the effects of the great depression, the macro economy adjusts to a much lower level of general equilibrium, where the aggregate demand conditions can never re-adjust to their prior levels because the macro economy is fundamentally different than before.

When millennials complain that they cannot find decent career opportunities in the bifurcated economy, they are partially accurate.

The rate of economic growth in the gig economy is too low because of the diversion of capital from the macro economy to the global corporations.

As a result of cronyism, there are two economies, one that represents the entire statistical benefits of economic growth, and one where statistics on GDP do not capture the economic malaise.

The millennial labor force is not plugged into the good jobs in the global crony capitalist system, they are plugged into the "gig" economy that features low wages and few health benefits.

There are no career portals of entry for millennials from the gig economy into the good jobs in the global corporate crony economy.

The three main components of the American global crony national economic structure are:

1. The global firms in the military-industrial complex.
2. The global manufacturing industrial firms with a financial interest in obtaining foreign trade benefits, especially with China.
3. The global banking and investment firms who coordinate global financial transactions in conjunction with global central banks.

The common characteristic of global cronyism, in all three of the national economic structures, is a preference for globalism, as opposed to promotion of a sovereign national economic interest.

Like the top-down, one party political system in China, the American global corporate crony political system is a one party top down system, based in Washington, that functions entirely independent of the consent of the governed.

Matthew Mitchell, in Uncontestable Favoritism, describes the power of the political coalition between corporate and government elites in terms of setting the economic priorities of the nation, much like the CCP of China.

Mitchell notes,

> "One of the most discussed of these institutions is agenda-setting power (Plott and Levine 1978; McKelvey 1976, 1979; Romer and Rosenthal 1978). Agenda setters such as standing committee chairs, calendar chairs, and chamber leaders are able to determine which bills get a floor vote as well as the order in which bills are considered. The literature has long emphasized that such rules permit a few powerful agenda setters to steer the process to their liking." (Mitchell, Matthew D., Uncontestable Favoritism Public Choice, Forthcoming. July 9, 2018. Available at SSRN).

Todd Zywicki places cronyism into an economic exchange framework to demonstrate that that the parties who benefit from the crony exchange exploit those who bear the costs of cronyism.

Zywicki states,

> "In the (implicit crony) exchange, the firm promises to share some of that surplus with politically-favored groups, such as labor unions or favored interest groups (such as environmental groups), and with the politicians themselves through campaign contributions and other means of support. Thus, the firms and their managers and shareholders gain what amounts to a sinecure and protection from the gales of creative destruction, and in exchange politicians can divert some of this flow of resources to their preferred policies and groups. (Todd J. Zywicki, Rent-Seeking, Crony Capitalism, and the Crony Constitution, Supreme Court Economic Review, Forthcoming; George Mason Legal Studies Research Paper No. LS 15-08; George Mason Law & Economics Research Paper No. 15-26. August 26, 2015. Available at SSRN).

In Zywicki's concept of the exchange, the political elites and corporate elites extract value from the rest of the economy, who are not a part of the crony system.

As Zywicki explains,

> "This power (of the elites) to single out certain parties for particular positive or negative treatment based on idiosyncratic political influence rather than principled (price-based) distinctions is a necessary condition for rent-seeking to occur, as the favored group must have some disadvantaged group that provides the gains."

Angelo Codevilla has described the one party politics of American global cronyism by calling it "America's Ruling Class."

Codevilla explains,

> "No one in a position of power in either party or with a national voice would take their objections seriously, that decisions about their money were being made in bipartisan backroom deals with interested parties, and that the laws on these matters were being voted by people who had not read them, the term "political class" came into use...our ruling class grew and set itself apart from the rest of us by its connection with ever bigger government, and above all by a certain attitude." (Angelo Codevilla, America's Ruling Class And the Perils of Revolution. July 16, 2010).

The propaganda of the ruling political class is that the elites know better than common citizens what promotes social welfare, and must, therefore, have the unchecked power to exploit the production value of the non-elites in order to obtain the revenue to achieve better social welfare outcomes in fairness and income equality.

As Codevilla notes,

> "The elite's attitude (of moral superiority) is key to understanding our bipartisan ruling class. Its first tenet is that "we" are the best and brightest while the rest of Americans are retrograde, racist, and dysfunctional unless properly constrained...Our ruling class's agenda is power for itself."

The identification of American one party rule was popularized by George Wallace, in 1966, when he proclaimed,

> "There's not a dime's worth of difference between the Democrat and Republican parties,"

Wallace would have been more accurate if he had identified the connection between the political elites, in both parties, and the corporate elites as collaborating to maintain political power to skew the entire economic structure to their own financial benefit.

Marcus Hawkins, in his article, "What Is the GOP Establishment? (January 28, 2020), drew a historical parallel between the ruling class in England and the Republican Party establishment, in America.

Hawkins noted,

> "The establishment within the Republican party tends to control the rules of the party system, party elections, and funding disbursements. The establishment is typically viewed as more elitist, politically moderate, and out of touch with true conservative voters."

The Republican establishment promotes the interests of large global corporations and is heavily influenced by the lobbying efforts of the Business Roundtable and the US Chamber of Commerce.

The Republican Party establishment collaborates with the Democrat Party elites in a system widely called "the swamp."

On the corporate side of the swamp are the three primary industrial sectors of the military industrial complex, the large global manufacturing firms that benefit from global trade, and the global financial banks.

On the government agency side of the swamp are the agents in the deep state military spy apparatus and Department of State that collaborate with elected government officials to promote the elite perspective on the U. S. role in the global economy.

On the legal institutional side are the law firms and judicial activist lobbying firms who do the lobbying and write the draft legislation to enact trade laws and tax policies that tend to establish monopolies and monopsonies by legal fiat.

The one party ruling class in America looks like, and functions like, the CCP in China that directs economic wealth to the cronies in the political system.

As Leonard Lynn and Hal Salzman note in "Collaborative Advantage,"

> "U. S. multinationals are weakening their national identities, becoming citizens of the countries in which they do business and

providing no favors to their country of origin. This means that the goal advocated by some U.S. policymakers of having the United States regain its position of leadership in all key technologies is simply not feasible, nor is it clear how the United States would retain that advantage when its firms are only loosely tied to the country." (Issues In Science and Technology, Winter 2006).

"Loosely tied" in their language means the same thing, economically, as disconnected in the language of regional input-output analysis.

When the large U. S. corporations moved their regional intermediate supply chains to China, they disconnected themselves from the national economy, and functioned more as "citizens of the world" than American corporate citizens, with an allegiance to the welfare of the U. S. economy.

Stephen Haber emphasizes the legal change in property rights granted to the participants in the global corporate crony system that skews the benefits exclusively to those agents.

Haber states,

"The preferential subsidies, monopoly rights or protection from international competition benefits global corporations by establishing a legal system that provides access to bank credit,, property rights protection between incumbents and new entrants and favorable trade agreements, like NAFTA." (Stephen Haber, Introduction: The Political Economy of Crony Capitalism, 2015).

The important point Haber is making is that the benefits of global crony capitalism system do not represent a zero sum outcome for millennials, who are not plugged into the global system.

The global crony capitalists cannot obtain their privileges and benefits without inflicting economic damage on the rest of the economy.
Zywicki places the macro economic effects of cronyism into the traditional economic benefit-cost framework by stating,

"So long as the cost of an interest group's investment in political lobbying activity is less than the expected benefit that the interest group can gain by lobbying the government for favorable treatment, the interest group will find it profitable to divert resources from productive uses that have a net benefit to society and the economy to lobbying expenditures aimed at merely redistributing wealth from less-organized interests to that interest group. (Zywicki, 2015).

The political and financial elites use legislation aimed at promoting the social welfare function of the corporate elites, as if that collectivist welfare function acts as a surrogate for a national welfare function.

In the language of national social welfare outcomes, the winners of crony corporatism can never compensate the losers because the exclusive benefits obtained by crony capitalists are not greater than the economic damage the crony system inflicts on the entire national economy.

As mentioned above, one macro economic effect that U. S. global corporations have had on the U. S. domestic economic structure is the offshoring of regional intermediate demand supply chains that were formerly in U. S. metro regions.

Those metro regional value chains used to service and support the larger corporations when production and innovation occurred in the domestic U. S. economy.

The value chains of the large corporations distributed income and employment multiplier effects throughout the economy.

The distributional income and multiplier effects no longer occur in America because the regional value chains are now located in regions like Bangalore and Shanghai.

Aligica and Tarko cite the loss of the income and employment multiplier effects as one reason why wealth in America has become more concentrated at the top of society, since the advent of global corporate cronyism.

In the absence of income and employment multiplier networks, there is no economic mechanism for the wealth at the top to "trickle down" to the gig economy.

As Aligca and Tarko state,

> "Cronyism is one cause of wealth inequality, and it has likely increased over time as the government has grown."

In place of the former market price based income and multiplier networks that distributed wealth, Ryan Bourne and Chris Edwards explain that the government welfare policies have stepped in to fill the void created when the supply chains left for China.

As they state,

> "The growing welfare state has increased wealth inequality. Government programs for retirement, healthcare, and other benefits have reduced the incentives and the ability of nonwealthy households to accumulate savings and thus have increased wealth inequality." (Bourne, Ryan and Edwards, Chris, Exploring Wealth Inequality Policy, Analysis No. 881, Cato Institute. November 20, 2019. Available at SSRN).

The loss of the metro value chains is one reason why millennials cannot find career opportunities in the crony economy.

In the prior period of time, before off shoring, most of the entry portals for good jobs occurred in the metro service and supply chains.

The metro value chains were also the source of most technological innovation in the American economy, which subsequently, was the major cause of national economic growth.

In their research on the relationship between young high growth firms and GDP, "Where Has All the Skewness Gone? The Decline in High-Growth (Young) Firms in the U.S.", Decker, Ryan & Haltiwanger,et.al., traced the decline to around 2000, about the same time that U. S. corporations began shipping intermediate supply chains to China.

They state,

> "Since 2000, the decline in dynamism and entrepreneurship has been accompanied by a decline in high-growth young firms. Prior research has shown that the sustained contribution of business startups to job creation stems from a relatively small fraction of high-growth young firms. The presence of these high-growth young firms contributes to a highly (positively) skewed firm growth rate distribution...
> In addition, key sectors have exhibited a sharp decline in positive skewness in the post-2000 period—specifically the high tech sector. This sector exhibited an increase in dispersion and skewness in firm growth rates

during the 1990s before the sharp decline. (Ryan A. Decker, John Haltiwanger, Ron S. Jarmin, Javier Miranda, Where Has All The Skewness Gone? The Decline In High-Growth (Young) Firms In The U.S., NBER Working Paper No. 21776. Revised in January 2016).

To answer their question about where the young high growth technology firms went, they went to China and India, along with the intermediate demand chains.

Most of the radical product innovation that occurred in the regional value chains were a result of technology collaboration between small high industrial firms in the 200 metro regions.

When the crony capitalist corporations exported the domestic supply chains, they permanently damaged America's great initial factor endowment of technology innovation.

Diagram 2 describes the same period of time, from 1996 to 2013, to show that very young firms contribute the most to economic growth. Over time, the young firms die, and as a result of off shoring the value chains, the older firms are not being replaced, causing national economic slow growth.

Diagram 2.

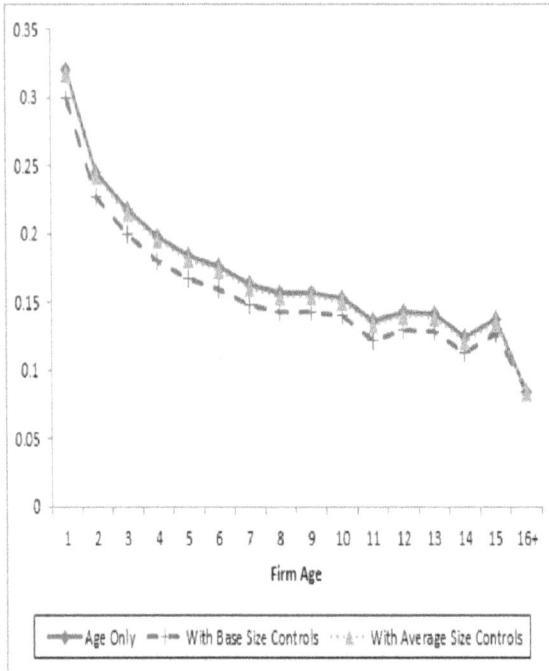

Figure 8 Output High Growth Firms by Firm Age, 1996-2013

Source: Statistics computed from the Revenue enhanced LBD subset 1996-2000, 2003-2013. Reported are estimated effects of linear probability models on controls as listed. All coefficients are reported relative to unconditional mean for 16+.

The permanent economic damage to the macro economy from crony corporate capitalism, beginning around 2001, is that the global corporations ate the seed corn of new venture creation and technology innovation in the national economy.

The damage caused to technology innovation by exporting the intermediate demand chains occurred in the "knowledge creation-knowledge diffusion process among small manufacturing firms.

As described by Jörg Thomä and Volker Zimmermann, small firms learn by doing, while larger global firms learn through more formal research that results in codified knowledge.

As applied to small firms, they note the importance of tacit knowledge creation in the process of technological innovation,

> "The focus is on experience-based knowledge and collaboration with customers, suppliers or competitors rather than in-house R&D activities. Small firm (DUI) learning often results in incremental innovation instead of disruptive innovation. Moreover, interaction between people and departments within the firm holds particular relevance for innovation success in the DUI mode."(Thomä, Jörg and Zimmermann, Volker, Non-R&D, Interactive Learning and Economic Performance: Revisiting Innovation in Small and Medium Enterprises). ifh Working Paper No. 17/2019. September 6, 2019. Available at SSRN).

Following the distinction between sustaining and radical innovation, made by Clayton Chistensen, the tacit knowledge of the small firms, gained in their service and supply chains, tends to result in more radical innovation than the sustaining innovation in larger firms, that aims at making existing products more user friendly.

Jorg and Zimmermann state,

> "Innovations in the (smaller), customer-oriented DUI group are often already associated with higher degrees of novelty. The practical skills and experienced-based knowledge of vocationally-trained workers also plays an important role in this context. A typical example of this learning mode are small craft-based SMEs that concentrate on niche markets and their capacity for customisation to compensate for disadvantages associated with small size." (2019).

It was this ability of small American firms in each metro region to create new radical products that was permanently damaged when the global crony corporations moved the intermediate demand chains to China.

In the absence of small firm technological innovation in America, new future markets were not created, and in the absence of new future markets, upward social mobility in America stagnated.

When millennials complain that the existing economy is not generating upward social mobility, they are correct.

In addition to damaging the rate of technological innovation on a macro basis, the off shoring of intermediate demand chains permanently damaged the metro regional economies in the 200 metro regions.

As a consequence, the elected leaders of the metro regions turned to providing industrial recruitment incentives to large corporations to induce them to locate part of their operations in the region. The incentives fit into the classification scheme as micro cronyism, provided by Aligca and Tarko.

The proponents of cronyism support the use of incentives, as a necessary part of creating economic growth in the metro regions.

Opponents of the use of tax incentives to recruit global corporations argue that the incentives are unconstitutional. (Vass, Laurie Thomas, Do targeted tax incentives used for industrial recruitment serve the public purpose: the trouble with the Maready ruling on industrial recruitment incentives. UNC Library. Carolina Collection, 1996).

The damage macro cronyism caused to technology innovation, by exporting the intermediate demand chains, occurred in the "knowledge creation-knowledge diffusion process among small manufacturing firms. (Vass, Laurie Thomas, Knowledge Creation and Knowledge Diffusion In Technology Evolution Forthcoming in The Theory of Technology Evolution, Chapter 7. January 9, 2019. Available at SSRN).

By getting rid of the disruptive innovation of small firms in metro regions, the large corporations were able to solidify their grip on the entire process of technological innovation in America, that features codified knowledge creation, primarily in universities. (Vass, Laurie Thomas, Do Cities Still Matter? The Economic Strength of Cities and the Economic Failure of Globalism in Promoting Regional Technological Innovation and Economic Prosperity. April 20, 2013. Available at SSRN).

The three primary industrial groups engaged in crony corporate capitalism are the military industrial corporations, the pharmaceutical and medical technology corporations, and the large international banking and investment firms.

All of the industrial groups share a common preference for globalism, and that common preference acts to damage domestic economic growth.

Pfizer is representative of how the preference for globalism works in the pharmaceutical group. In his recent investigative article "Pfizer To Ax It Contractors," Lee Howard reports on how Pfizer's global innovation platform works to damage American workers. (TheDay.com, November, 2008).

Howard writes,

> "Pfizer Inc. has been training foreign workers in Groton and New London over the past few months inanticipation of transferring much of its information-technology work from local contractors to outside contracting firms...

The new policy, known internally as Procedure 117, will force many of these contractors, some of whom have been working at Pfizer's local campuses for a decade or more, to leave by the end of this year. Foreign workers from India and China, are brought to the U. S. for training. They are then sent back to their home communities, and their work replaces the work done by American workers, who assisted the foreign workers in the training project."

In contrast to replacing middle class workers with foreign workers in the cronyism of pharmaceuticals, Coyne and Hall begin their research on the U. S. military industrial crony complex, by describing the extent of economic influence this industrial sector has on the entire U. S. macro economy.

They write,

"A review of the top 100 defense contractors for FY 2016 finds recipients from the following industries: aerospace, computer and technology, accounting and professional services, courier services, engineering and construction, finance and private equity, health care, higher education, and telecommunications. As this list suggests, the reach of state military activities into the private economy is anything but "minimal." (Coyne, Christopher J. and Hall, Abigail, Cronyism: Necessary for the Minimal, Protective State The Independent Review: A Journal of Political Economy, Forthcoming; GMU Working Paper in Economics No. 18-26. July 30, 2018. Available at SSRN).

One outcome of the military industrial crony complex are the endless wars, such as Afghanistan.

The wars financially benefit the corporations in the military industrial crony system, but inflict costs on the soldiers and the rest of the economy not plugged into the military industrial crony system.

In terms of wasting economic resources, they cite the case of Boeing's crony influence in producing the C-17. General Gates had told Congress that the C-17 was a wasteful project, and not needed to enhance the military readiness.

Coyne and Hall write,

> "Ignoring Gates, members of Congress ordered a further expansion of the fleet in order to direct benefits to their constituencies. Boeing, who manufactured the C-17,

estimated that the program supported 650 suppliers and over thirty thousand jobs across forty-four states (McCartney 2015: 41). While undertaken in the name of contributing to the nation's security, the reality is that the production of the C-17 became a "welfare program, offering profits for companies, jobs for workers and unions, and political support for cooperative lawmakers. Planes the Pentagon has not thought necessary have been built to promote the reelection of congressman and senators."

They conclude that the military industrial crony system in America reminds them of the corporate fascism of Germany, where Hitler allowed the private corporations to remain private, but directed them to produce the military goods that the Nazi regime required.

They write,

"The U.S. defense sector's public-private arrangements are more reminiscent of fascist economic systems than of competitive, private market (see Higgs 2012: 204-224). There is private ownership over the means of production, but the evolution and actions of the private owners are dictated by government mandates established by political authorities."

In their research on how macro cronyism affects the large corporation's financial performance, Russell S. Sobel and Rachel L. Graefe-Anderson found that only banks obtained a direct increase in corporate financial benefits from cronyism.

They state,

> "In this paper we estimate the extent to which industry-level and firm-level performance is determined by political connections rather than normal market forces. Our results suggest that corporate political activity is positively correlated with executive compensation measures, but not robustly with firm performance and profitability measures. In only the case of the banking and finance industries do we see any evidence that measures of firm financial performance are positively influenced by political activities. (Sobel, Russell and Graefe-Anderson, Rachel, The Relationship between Political Connections and the Financial Performance of Industries & Firms MERCATUS WORKING PAPER. (07/09/2014). Available at SSRN).

The other two main parts of the macro industrial sectors (military industrial and pharmaceutical manufacturing) did not benefit, as corporations, from the cronyism.

Rather, they found that the economic benefit flowed directly to the senior executives that managed the crony corporations.

They found that the ability of the banks to obtain corporate-level benefits stemmed from the bank's ability to eliminate smaller banks from competition, through political lobbying efforts.

They cite the example of how the large banks used the Dodd-Frank legislation as a political cover to eliminate the smaller banks.

They cite the case of JP Morgan, on how this process worked,

> "For example, JP Morgan Chase CEO Jamie Dimon observed that because of the aggregate costs of complying with all of the rules, regulations, and capital costs associated with Dodd-Frank, that JP Morgan has built a "bigger moat" between it and its smaller competitors."

In the case of banks, the cronyism works because one part of the swamp, the elected representatives, threaten to impose harm or take away benefits currently held by various banks, as Sobel and Graefe-Anderson state, by obtaining "tribute" from the big banks.

They explain,

> "The law has imposed huge compliance costs on small banks and that they have been less able to bear those costs than large banks. Thus, large banks have grown still larger as smaller community banks have disappeared from the market under Dodd-Frank's regulatory burden."

Their research suggests that the financial benefits of both micro and macro cronyism are obtained by a very narrow set of corporate executives.
They state,

> "Thus, our main finding suggests that the top executives of firms are the ones who are able to capture the benefits of firm political connections across firms in the United States… We find a robust and significant positive relationship between political activity and executive compensation. Therefore, while industry and firm-level performance are not robustly related to "cronyism," executive compensation is suggesting that any benefits gained from corporate political activity are largely captured by firm executives."

Part of the millennial attraction socialism is based upon the objective, observable fact that the global corporate elite are inflicting economic damage on the rest of society in a selfish effort to direct financial benefits to themselves.

This behavior of the American crony elite system resembles the behavior of Chinese elites who direct benefits to themselves and their cronies.

The entire American crony political and economic system becomes oriented to obtaining privileges rather than maximizing profits.

Macro economic cronyism feeds on itself and becomes a self-fulfilling process where corporate elites who benefit from the system become political advocates of the system in Congress.

The global crony economy is stable and resolute from displacement.

Mathew Mitchell cites his research that describes the self-fulfilling process of cronyism, which permanently damages the constitutional system of citizen democracy in America.

> "Our research shows that business leaders who benefit from government favoritism are more comfortable with government intervention into markets. We surveyed 500

American business leaders. What we found was that capitalists who benefit from government favoritism are more likely to accept interventions into markets. Being a favorite is correlated with approving of favoritism." (Mitchell, Matthew D., Uncontestable Favoritism Public Choice, July 9, 2018. Available at SSRN).

As Haber, (2002), notes, the economic loss to society results primarily from a change of legal property rights corruptly obtained by the elite, through Congressional legislation.

Any change in the legal status quo of privileges of the elites would upset the equilibrium of the crony corporate system.

Haber states,

> "Any unexpected change of policies would have a negative effect on the wealth and happiness of crucial members of the political elite. Thus, the system of property rights remains stable as long as the political elites do not change and the commitment (of the elites to the status quo) problem is solved if they are sufficiently integrated with the economic sector."

Part of the millennial attraction to socialism is based upon the false equivalency that crony capitalism is authentic legitimate free enterprise capitalism.

The millennials can easily see the defects of crony corporatism and falsely believe that socialism would be a better, more fair, solution.

Millennials equate authentic free enterprise capitalism with crony capitalism because that is what they have been taught in public schools.

Crony capitalism fits with the Marxist concept of capitalist class exploitation, and that propaganda of crony capitalism supports the political agenda of socialists.

Zywicki explains the distinction between crony capitalism and free competitive enterprise, by noting,

> "As used here, cronyism describes a system in which government, big business, and powerful interest groups (especially labor unions) work together to further their joint interests. Government protects and subsidizes powerful corporations and in (implicit) exchange the government uses those businesses to carry out government policies

outside of the ordinary processes of government... The term is misleading, of course, because "crony capitalism" has little to do with capitalism, and is actually its opposite. What has come to be known as "crony capitalism" has traditionally and perhaps more accurately been known as "corporatism"—a system where businesses are privately owned, but there is a comprehensive intertangling of government and private industry, such that the success of various firms or industries is closely tied to government and government frequently uses private industry to directly or indirectly accomplished preferred political goals." (Zywicki, 2015).

Zywicki's analysis of the exchange relationships in cronyism provides an insight into how the Chinese system of communist cronyism resembles the American system of global corporate cronyism.

In both cases, the elites must exploit profits from the rest of the economy.

Zywicki states,

"This power to single out certain parties for particular positive or negative treatment based on idiosyncratic political influence rather than principled distinctions is a necessary condition for rent-seeking to occur, as the favored group must have some disadvantaged group that provides the gains."

In the millennial's attraction to socialism, it does not seem logical that the millennials would exchange one form of crony capitalist exploitation for another form of crony capitalist exploitation.

As Zywicki notes, in both Chinese and American cronyism, the elites "must have some disadvantaged groups that provide the gains."

The legitimacy of the millennial's complaints about the unfair outcomes of crony capitalism are valid.

But, the better solution is not more power in the hands of corporate or political elites.

The better solution is to extend the benefits of the American free enterprise entrepreneurial economy to the 350 metro regions who were damaged by globalism.

Chapter 4. The European Crony Socialist Economy.

In many respects, the defects in the European technology innovation system are the same as those in China.

The policy response in both economies is also the same, which means stealing American technology.

In China, the rules on global trading require trading partners to license technology to the Chinese national champions, so that the Chinese military can steal the technology through reverse engineering.

The Europeans also steal American technology, but in a very sophisticated legal gambit that they call "interoperability," which means that U. S. technology must operate on European components.

In its 2004 decision against Microsoft, the Commission of the European Communities, based its ruling on the term "interoperability." (Case COMP/C-3/37.792 Microsoft, Brussels, April 21, 2004).

According to the legal analysis provided by Daniel F. Spulber,

> "The Commission's decision turns on the meaning of a single critical word: interoperability." (Competition Policy and the Incentive to Innovate: The Dynamic Effects of Microsoft v. Commission, Yale Journal on Regulation, Volume 25, Number 2, Summer 2008).

The economic logic under girding the Microsoft decision is supportive of the European model of innovation, which is more communal, collaborative, and collectivist in its implementation than the current U. S. model of innovation.

Like the technology innovation process in both China and the U. S. crony system, the European technology innovation replaces innovation based upon tacit knowledge with formal university research that results in codified knowledge.

The U. S. model is more individualistic, and features rewards to innovation based upon individual appropriation of incomes and profits, especially those related to intellectual property rights.

The U. S. model is more heavily based upon the creation and diffusion of tacit knowledge, gained in small enterprise social and business networks.

The logic of the European Commission's Microsoft decision, in the short term, makes good economic and political sense. European-style innovation tends to preserve the economic status quo economic equilibrium at low levels of economic growth. European sustaining innovation does not overturn political equilibrium and the main beneficiaries of sustaining innovation in Europe are the very large global corporations, who engage in most of the sustaining innovation. (Vass, Laurie Thomas, The Economic and Political Consequences of European-Style Innovation Policy. November 10, 2008. Available at SSRN).

The entire population of large EU global firms is only about 463. The entire economic growth and technology innovation depend on the fortunes of these 463 firms.

Out of a total workforce of 235 million, about 50% work in government or wholesale trade.

There are only around 58 million workers that are not directly dependent on state payments for income in some shape or form.

The European Commission decision in the Microsoft case shows one interpretation of promoting the sovereign EU economic interest.

The Commission intends to protect the large crony socialist corporations, through a legal mandate that leads to macro economic decline.

New markets created by technology innovation tend to destroy the status quo distributions of income, wealth, and political power.

Schumpeter called the effects of this type of radical innovation the "winds of creative destruction," and the very last thing the European Commission wants to see are any economic winds of creative destruction that upset the economic status quo equilibrium for their large corporations.

The Commission's mandate for technological interoperability represents a shift from an earlier focus on economic growth to a focus on income redistribution, via a thinly-veiled technology transfer trade policy.

Their mandate on interoperability is political rent-seeking on a massive global scale.

The flaw in the EU logic on interoperability is that the technology transfer obtains sustaining innovation, not radical new product innovation.

Sustaining technology innovation does not add technological diversity, which is the main ingredient to radical innovation.

Spulber notes,

> "Government takings of intellectual property appear to some policy makers as less egregious than takings of physical property... It appears to be a public benefit to release intellectual goods from (U.S.) private ownership, thereby conferring on everyone the benefits of non-rivalrous consumption. In other words, the European mandate for interoperability is rent-seeking for the masses."

The crony socialist model in the EU is to use government to benefit a narrow spectrum of companies that are incapable of creating economic growth.

One effect of stealing American technology is that the corporations conduct very little formal R & D, anymore.

As Spulber notes,

> "Why invest in costly R&D when you can get it for free from the leading company (U. S.) in your industry? Simply send the leading company a request for the use of any and all of

its innovations.. the European Commission used Microsoft's desire for market access as the ploy to impose its mandate. In other words, promotion of innovation policy in Europe was connected to a judicial ruling on trade policy through the mandate of interoperability in order to benefit European corporations."

Applied world-wide, forcing disclosure of American private technology in the European approach to innovation leads to global economic collapse and global political rent-seeking.

This is the ultimate economic and political consequence of European-style innovation policy. (Vass, 2008).

The main macro economic cost of European cronyism is that the EU rate of GDP growth is permanently lower because cronyism diverts scarce resources into non-productive enterprises, which are based upon political relationships, and are not based upon market prices.

As is the case for U. S. global corporate cronyism that leads to increasing wealth inequality among social classes, the European social welfare model of innovation leads to permanent wealth inequality, with limited opportunity for upward social class mobility.

The academic and political elites in the EU are aware of the lack of upward social class mobility.

The OECD report on social mobility reported that one in three children with a low-earning father will stay trapped on low earnings, while most of the other two-thirds will only move one rung up the income scale during their lifetime.

Gabriela Ramos, OECD chief of staff, stated,

> "Too many people feel they are being left behind and their children have too few chances to get ahead. We need to ensure that everyone has the opportunity to succeed, especially the most disadvantaged, and that growth becomes truly inclusive." (Eurofound Social mobility in the EU, Publications Office of the European Union, Luxembourg, 2017).

The EU report on social mobility explains that citizens across the EU have become increasingly concerned that young people will have fewer opportunities for upward social mobility than their parents or even their grandparents.

The report states that,

> "Younger generations of men and women ...
> are less likely to experience upward mobility
> and more likely to experience downward
> mobility'(Goldthorpe, 2016, pp. 95–96).

Ramos misdiagnoses the economic problem in the
EU. The problem is not social inclusivity.

The problem is that high EU taxes cause low EU
economic growth. Low economic growth causes EU
social class stagnation.

In their 2015 research, Fessler and Schurz used a
large survey database across European countries to
explore the relationship between the level of social
spending and wealth distribution.

Their statistical results showed that "the degree of
welfare state spending across countries is negatively
correlated with household net wealth." (Pirmin
Fessler and Martin Schürz, Private Wealth Across
European Countries: The Role of Income,
Inheritance and the Welfare State. Eurosystem
Working Paper Series, September 2105).

They explained that increases in government welfare
spending increased wealth inequality, but
predominantly in the lower income classes.

The EU upper classes benefit from the EU crony capitalist system, and are immune from the damage to the lower social classes.

As they stated,

> "The substitution effect of welfare state expenditures with regard to private wealth holdings is significant along the full net wealth distribution, but is relatively lower at higher levels of net wealth. Given an increase in welfare state expenditure, the percentage decrease in net wealth of poorer households is relatively stronger than for households in the upper part of the wealth distribution...
> This finding implies that given an increase of welfare state expenditure, wealth inequality measured by standard relative inequality measures, such as the Gini coefficient, will increase."

The economic consequence of increased welfare spending in the EU is not limited to increasing wealth inequality, the tax diversion of surplus capital from corporations and households decreases the amount of capital available for technology innovation.

Gary Galles describes the diversion of profits to social welfare spending as the "crowding out" effect.

He states,

> "One cost of these programs is that they undermine the incentives and the means for people to accumulate personal savings. Effectively, they displace or "crowd out" wealth-building by households, particularly those with moderate incomes. (Gary Galles, Why the Cost of Government Is Higher Than You Think, Mises Daily Articles. May 2014).

The main effect of crowding out on technology innovation in the EU is that the potential amount of venture capital available for investment in new ventures is crowded out by the increased social welfare spending.

The only source of economic growth and capital investment in the EU are the 463 large corporations, who have established a legal state monopoly on technology innovation.

According to the 2016 FORBES Global 2000, the 463 Europe-based public companies, had profits of $493 billion, on gross revenues of $9.7 trillion.

The very low rate of net profits to revenues is due to the very high rates of taxation in the EU.

In other words, the high rate of taxation "crowds out" capital that otherwise would be available for technology innovation and new venture creation.

In 2017, taxes on capital, which include taxes on the capital income of households and corporations and on capital stocks, represented 8.6 % of EU GDP, a higher rate of capital tax than in 2008.

In 2017, taxes and compulsory actual social contributions in the 28 Member States of the European Union accounted for 39 % of gross domestic product (GDP), about 12% higher than in the U. S.

For the past 13 years, the average annual rate of venture capital investment in the EU has been about $3 billion.

As a result of the low rate of capital investment, the rate of GDP growth in the EU has stagnated.

The EU crony socialist system concentrates the power to make investment and tax decisions in a very small set of political and financial elites.

The entire crony system is designed to protect the privileged status quo of the 463 large corporations.

Diagram 3. Describes the low, but stable rate of capital investment in the EU, for a ten-year period of time.

The rate of capital investment was about $3 billion.

Venture capital funds raised (billion euro) in the EU and in the United States, 2007-2016

■ United States ■ EU (1)

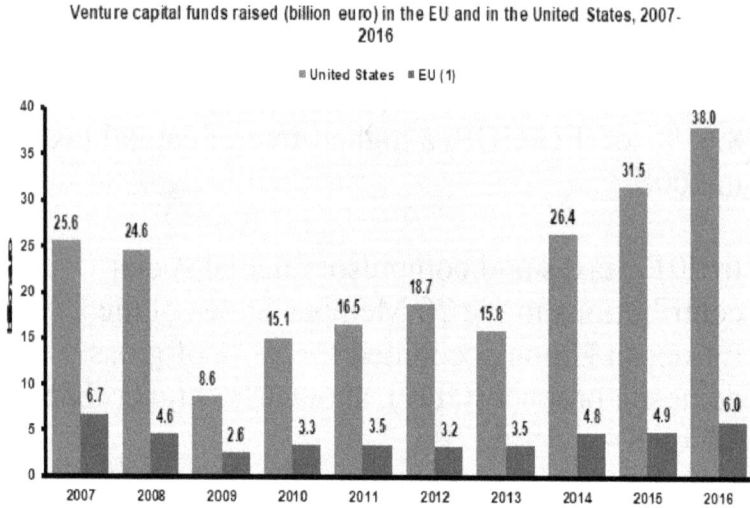

Image: Invest Europe, NVCA/Pitchbook/DG Research and Innovation - Unit for Analysis and Monitoring of National Research and Innovation Policies.

The low rate of capital investment resulted in a low rate of high growth firms, commonly called "unicorns."

In 2017, the EU managed to create only 26 high growth technology firms, called "Unicorns."

Most of the economic growth in the EU comes from these high growth firms.

That rate of new, high technology venture creation is inadequate to provide economic growth and upward social class mobility for the EU.

Diagram 4.

Number of unicorns, December 2017

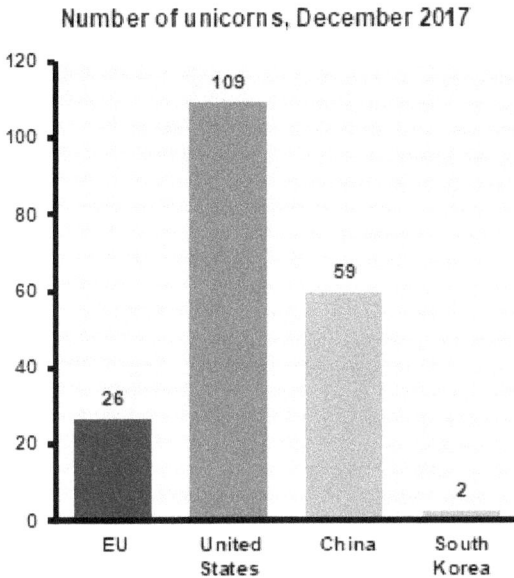

The rate of GDP growth in the EU is loo low to create job opportunities and upward mobility for the social classes because the EU crony system is incapable of generating radical technology innovation.

Rather than addressing the dysfunction in technology innovation, the policy response of the EU has been to cut interest rates in order to stimulate aggregate demand.

But, the problem of inadequate GDP growth is not related to the supply of credit, it is related to a lack of domestic capital investment in new ventures.

Diagram 5.

European Union GDP Growth Rate

Summary   Forecast   Stats   Download ▾

3Y   10Y   25Y   MAX   Chart   Compare   Export   API   Embed

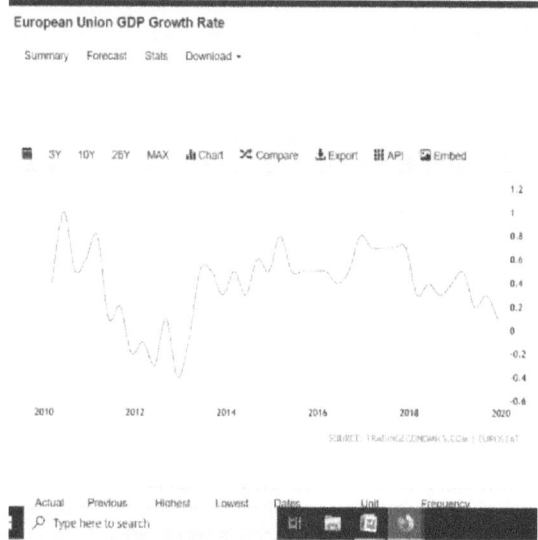

SOURCE: TRADINGECONOMICS.COM | EUROSTAT

Actual   Previous   Highest   Lowest   Dates   Unit   Frequency

The European Union economy grew by just 0.1 percent on quarter in the last three months of 2019, easing from a 0.3 percent expansion in the previous period.
Image: binsights/OECD/Eurostat/DG Research and Innovation - Unit for Analysis and Monitoring of National Research and Innovation Policies

Cutting interest rates, below zero, in the EU is an odd, counter-logical, policy response to low GDP growth, made even more odd by the fact that the EU policy and political elites are aware of the solution.

In their detailed economic report, Science, Research and Innovation Performance of the EU 2018, Key Findings. (European Commission Directorate-General for Research and Innovation), they begin with the correct diagnosis of their economic problems.

They state,

> "Innovation is a fundamental driver of economic and social prosperity. It boosts economic growth, creates new and better jobs, enables social mobility, fights climate change and im-proves the overall quality of life. Raising prosperity levels has always been closely associated with the capacity of the economies to create and diffuse innovations."

They continue with the correct conclusion about why economic growth has stagnated,

> "Sluggish productivity growth and weak diffusion of innovation are holding back more resilient economic growth. This

stagnation in productivity is occurring despite the rise of many breakthrough technologies such as the Internet of Things, robotics and artificial intelligence... Europe is failing to transform its high scientific excellence into leadership in innovation and entrepreneurship."

The EU elites cannot bring themselves to admit the reality that their crony socialist system, that protects the 463 large corporations, is the wrong platform for entrepreneurial new venture creation.

The solution to their economic problems is a much greater rate of private capital investment in new ventures, which can only happen if the supply of capital increases, which can only happen if they reduce government expenditures on social welfare programs.

Gabriela Ramos, OECD chief of staff, thinks the EU economic problems may be related to "inclusivity."

She needs to go back and re-read the great European economist, Joseph Schumpeter, to get a better idea on what creates an entrepreneurial economy.

American millennials who are attracted to the European crony socialist model would do well to examine the defects and flaws in their system that results in static social class mobility, where 1 in 3 low class workers never break out of their position at birth.

Chapter 5. The American Free Enterprise Entrepreneurial Economy.

Millennials confront a mutually exclusive choice about the economic future that they will support

They can choose to embrace one of the three crony systems that exploit profits of non-elites, or they can embrace an individualistic entrepreneurial free enterprise system, where entrepreneurs appropriate the value of the production that they create.

In contrast to the centralized elite, top down decision making in the three crony systems, the free enterprise economy is decentralized, democratic, and based upon continuous innovation.

The entrepreneurial economy occurs in major metro regions, not centralized in New York and Washington.

Consequently, national aggregate statistics, like GDP and interest rates do not capture the economic dynamics of the innovation economy.

The data that is used to measure the rate of innovation at the regional metro level are indicators like the rate of new venture creation, the rate of intellectual patents, or the rate of venture capital investment.

As the research by Decker, Ryan & Haltiwanger, et.al., (2017), indicate, since 2001, the U.S. entrepreneurial economy has not been growing like the period before the off shoring began.

They state,

> "The pace of business dynamism and entrepreneurship in the U.S. has declined over recent decades. We show that the character of that decline changed around 2000. Since 2000 the decline in dynamism and entrepreneurship has been accompanied by a decline in high-growth young firms."

The reason for the weakness in new venture creation is that the American corporate crony capitalist system is damaging the rate of new venture creation and technological innovation in the major metro regions.

Millennials cannot have both the consumer benefits of the global macro economic structure of corporate cronyism and, at the same time, enjoy the high economic growth rates of the entrepreneurial economy.

Crony capitalism cannot function without diverting capital resources away from entrepreneurial innovation, which the crony capitalists do not control, to the corporate innovation and technology, that they do control.

In other words, the choice millennials confront is either a global economy with slow economic growth and lack of upward occupational mobility in the 3 crony systems, (Chinese crony capitalism, EU crony socialism, and corporate crony capitalism) or rapid growth and new job creation in the entrepreneurial economy.

American crony capitalism is emerging as the most important barrier to the emergence of democratic, decentralized entrepreneurial capitalism.

There are two major sources of conflict between crony capitalism and the entrepreneurial economy.

The two major sources of clonflict can be broken down further into four areas of cultural and political conflict of interest between the goals of global crony capitalism and the metro regional free enterprise innovation economy.

In each conflict, the crony capitalists gain an advantage because of their political influence in skewing the laws and regulation to their exclusive benefit.

Two Major Conflicts Cultural/political values.	Individual freedom, reward based upon individual merit, maximum individual risk-taking.	Globalist/collectivist values oriented to using government to promote resolution of market-based conflicts.

The first of the four subordinate conflicts is over open or closed, proprietary information flows between small firms and global large firms in metro industrial sectors.

The second conflict is over the labor market mobility between inter-corporate career transfers of scientific personnel between existing firms and the creation of new ventures,

Third, there is a conflict over the control of codified knowledge from universities to the large corporations, through technology licensing contracts, and the tacit knowledge creation in the metro regional intermediate demand chains.

Control over knowledge flows determines the path of technical change in the region. (Vass, Laurie Thomas, The Big Free Market Lie: How Control Over Regional Technological Innovation Is the Next Political Battleground For the Wealth of Nations. Great American Business and Economics Press, 2007. Available at UNC.edu Carolina Collection, Wilson Library).

Finally, there is a political conflict over whether collective, public welfare decisions will be based upon the cultural/political values regarding globalist/collectivist values, or the individualistic values of a representative democracy, individual freedom and financial rewards based upon individual merit.

The globalist laws and policies that were implemented in the early 1990's disproportionately served the financial interests of global corporations to the detriment to the citizens in metro regions in the United States.

Those laws and policies had the effect of creating legal monopolies that cut off the flow tacit knowledge in each metro region.

In the absence of open flows of tacit knowledge, the overall national macro rate of economic growth ratcheted down to a new low level of equilibrium.

The new low level of equilibrium created static social class mobility, where the elites grew richer and the rest of the citizens were consigned to the gig economy.

In contrast to the low levels of economic growth of crony capitalism, the economic growth caused by new venture technical change causes new income flows to be created where none had existed before.

Part of the new income is a result of increased productivity, meaning that output increases with reduced inputs in the production unit.

Part of the new income is in the form of profits related to new goods produced by new production units.

Another part of the income is in the form of wages and salaries paid to people who work in the new units.

The reason that the conflict over career mobility between the two economies is important is that the economic growth occurs as a result of an entrepreneur taking knowledge gained from using the old technology, in the old unit with her when she leaves to create the new unit.

Her intent in creating the new unit is to use the technical knowledge to build a new and better unit, a more efficient unit, than the old unit.

As a consequence of property rights in the entrepreneurial economy, the entrepreneur appropriates the value of her production, not the crony corporation or the state.

She also bears the risk of failure that her innovation will be a failure. The research by Decker, Ryan & Haltiwanger, et.al., (2017), indicate that 70% of the new ventures fail within the first five years.

The other 30% of new ventures are responsible for most of the economic growth in the economy.

As long as there is a continuous flow of new ventures coming into existence to replace the failed ventures, the macro economy continues to grow, and this is where the corporate crony system extracts its toll on the U. S. economy, and also in the EU.

As the research by Decker, Ryan & Haltiwanger, et.al., (2017), show, in U. S. crony capitalism, the rate of new venture creation, after eight years, is too low to sustain macro economic growth.

Diagram 6.

Figure 3: United States Quarterly Startups and Exits

~~ startups — exits

240K

220K

200K

180K

160K

1995   2000   2005   2010   2015

- In the third quarter of 2016, 240,000 establishments started up, generating 872,000 new jobs in the United States. Startups are counted when business establishments hire at least one employee for the first time. (Source: BDM)

- In the same period, 215,000 establishments exited resulting in 749,000 jobs lost. Exits occur when establishments go from having at least one employee to having none, and then remain closed for at least one year. (Source: BDM)

- Figure 3 displays quarterly startups and exits from 1992 to 2016. Each series is smoothed across multiple quarters to highlight long-run trends. (Source: BDM)

The BLS data covers only business establishments with employees. BLS refers to startups as births and exits as deaths. These terms are distinct from the BLS openings and closings categories. Openings include seasonal re-openings and closings include seasonal shutterings. Quarterly startup and exit values may not align with Figure 3 due to smoothing.

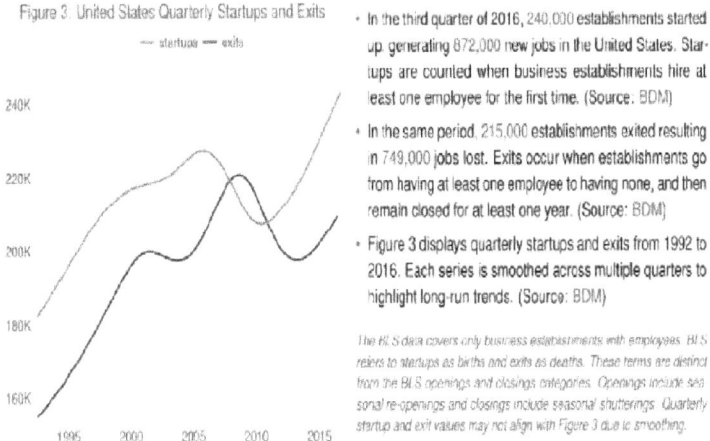

In China, the rate of new venture creation is too low because the CCP extorts all the profits and diverts them to cronies and state owned enterprises.

In the EU, government taxes crowd out the source of capital that could be used to create new ventures.

A total of 26 new ventures in the EU in 2017 is a ridiculously low number of new ventures for a population of 445 million citizens.

In the U. S., when the crony corporations off shored the intermediate demand supply chains to China and India, and they damaged the American initial factor endowment of individual enterprise for creating new ventures.

Most of the new venture creation in the U. S. occurs in 15 metro regions, and the policy goal for millennials who support of the entrepreneurial innovation economy is to extend the new venture creation model to the other 185 metro regions in the country.

In his research, The Top 15 Most Entrepreneurial Cities for 2018, Henry Kanapi, of fitsmallbusiness.com presents a map of the 15 most entrepreneurial metro regions (Starting a Business, Statistics, February 12, 2018).

All of the regions share a certain type of entrepreneurial culture, characterized by many periodic business social networking events, and angel capital conferences, where entrepreneurs make pitches to raise capital.

Diagram 7.

The Top 15 Most Entrepreneurial Cities for 2018

Denver
Aurora
Broomfield

Boston
Cambridge
Quincy

San Francisco
Oakland
Fremont

New York
Northern New
Jersey
Lond Island

Los Angeles
Long Beach
Santa Ana

Washington
Arlington
Alexandria

Carlsbad
San Marcos
San Diego

Atlanta
Sandy Springs
Marietta

Dallas
Fort Worth
Arlington

Orlando
Kissimmee
Sanford

Las Vegas
Paradise

Houston
Sugar Land
Bayton

Phoenix
Mesa
Glendale

Austin
Round Rock
San Marcos

Miami
Fort Lauderdale
Pompano Beach

FitSmallBusiness.com
Get Your Business Into Shape

To summarize the mutually exclusive choice for millennials about the most fair economy, the business-social network of entrepreneurs and venture capitalists in the 15 metro regions compete with the crony capitalist business-social networks in New York and Washington, comprised of members of the Business Roundtable and the U. S. Chamber of Commerce., the five investment and commercial bankers who are too big to fail, and senior management of corporations in the U. S. military industrial complex.

The metro regional social networks act to facilitate technical change, but are not organized as a special political interest group at the national level, like the crony corporate capitalists.

The crony network has financial interests in maintaining the status arrangement of power, at the national level.

One business social network promotes tacit knowledge creation and is characterized by unique cultural values associated with individual risk taking and creating new ventures.

The other network limits the spread of knowledge by obtaining closed proprietary research primarily from universities.

Richard Florida, in The Distinct Personality of Entrepreneurial Cities, (August 3, 2015), explains the connection between the entrepreneurial culture and tacit knowledge creation.

Florida states,

> "The entrepreneurial culture (an environment that fosters entrepreneurship) creates an economy where entrepreneurs have the drive and resilience to overcome obstacles, are more open to new ideas, and are able to connect with people, build and lead teams, and get things done... The entrepreneurial culture interacts with and connects to local (tacit) knowledge and talent. As Renfrow puts it, "new knowledge will have a greater propensity to generate entrepreneurship in regions with a pronounced entrepreneurial culture where the predominant attitudes and norms reinforce [SIC] individual's decisions to act upon entrepreneurial opportunities."

Pier Saviotti, in Technological Evolution, Variety and the Economy, (1996) states that innovating firms are not uniformly distributed across geographical territory. Innovative firms tend to be located near other innovative firms.

This tendency of firms to concentrate in a region contributes to the development of a regional macrotechnology, which is the same concept that Florida describes as an entrepreneurial culture.

According to Saviotti, the reason one metro region develops a macrotechnology as opposed to any other region is related to the,

> "...specific institutional configurations and by the cumulative, local, and specific character of the knowledge that the institutions possess."

The geographically-specific technological knowledge in a metro facilitates the ability of all the firms to absorb new technological knowledge.

In other words, an existing social-business network of skilled individuals, working in a similar technology production unit, share some specialized technical knowledge about a process.

Within this network, potential entrepreneurs meet with each other and discuss the feasibility of starting a new venture, based upon their shared technical knowledge and their understanding of the potential market for the products produced.

The entrepreneur provides an ingredient to the process of technical change that is absent in the framework of the crony capitalist corporate economy.

According to Robert McAdams, in Paths of Fire, (1996), the entrepreneurs have a "creative vision" in their capacity to anticipate a new convergence of consumer preferences and technological possibilities.

Peter Temin makes this same point in his article, "Entrepreneurs and Managers" (2000).

He states that

> "...entrepreneurs are the agents of change, ...(they) see new opportunities, invent new machines, discover new markets, ...(they)perform a different function from that of the manager, who works within a known technology, organization, and market."

In more common language, all of the engineers, scientists, mid-level managers in the region communicate with each other about how the new process is working, and when they leave to create their own new venture, it is that new process that forms the basis on their own equipment and machinery purchases.

In The Lever of Riches: Technological Creativity and Economic Progress, (1990), Joel Mokyr reviews the relationship between economic development and technological innovation by first raising the question why economic growth occurs in some societies and not in others.

According to Mokyr, economic growth results from open flows of innovation, which only occur under one configuration of constitutional rules advocated by Buchanan.

According to Mokyr, technological progress tends to occur in metro regional economies which have well-educated citizens, who are deeply engaged in the economic and political decisions of their communities.

In such a society, the appearance of technical progress is rapidly diffused, and as the knowledge embodied in the change spreads among citizens, it creates imbalances and bottlenecks in existing interindustry relations.

The entire process of economic growth caused by open flows of knowledge can be seen as the shifting of the national production function outward, which is reflected by changing technical coefficients in a dynamic input-output model the national economy.

Economic growth caused by technical change is a result of capital investments made by entrepreneurs in new production units create new interindustry relationships and new market relationships that did not exist before.

Brink Lindsey, of the Niskanen Center, (2017), aptly summarizes what has become a widespread consensus among scholars from many different fields within the economics profession:

> "The long-term future of economic growth hinges ultimately on innovation. Indeed, as Sachs and McArthur have stated, "The more we think about it, the more we realize that technological innovation is almost certainly the key driver of long-term economic growth."

Most of the radical innovation that creates new products and new future markets, occurs in metro regional economies, as a result of tacit knowledge creation and diffusion.

The metro regional economies that have the greatest technological diversity, where products from different genetic technological heredities are crossed, have the greatest rates of economic growth.

Diagram 8 describes the overlay between metro regions with industrial diversity and entrepreneurial culture. (CityLab, 2015).

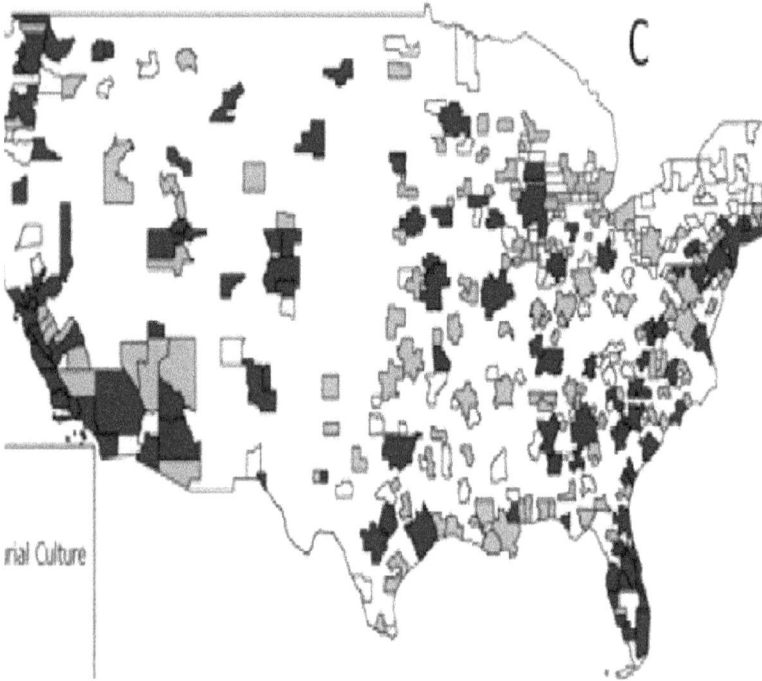

In all of the regions on the map, there is a potential for radical technology innovation, whose economic effect is totally unforeseen and unanticipated, and involves the emergence of entirely new final demand markets and brand new intermediate demand value chains.

Technological innovation cause those new markets to emerge, which then causes economic growth,

something that both Schumpeter and Solow have taught for nearly a century. (Vass, Laurie Thomas, The Theory of Technology Evolution, GabbyPress, 2017).

In making a choice between crony corporate capitalism and the American free enterprise entrepreneurial economy, millennials should recognize that a national innovation economic policy is required to confront the dominant crony capitalist policies.

If the millennials shift their allegiance from socialism to innovation, they can devote their energy to supporting this new national economic policy.

The national innovation economic policy is about increasing the rate of private capital investments in private new ventures, some of which may result in radical innovations.

Diagram 9 describes the relationship between private capital investment on a national scale. The diagram shows that as private domestic goes up, economic growth goes up. (St. Louis Federal Reserve, FRED, 2014).

Diagram 9.

The comovement of investment and GDP

Posted on June 19, 2014

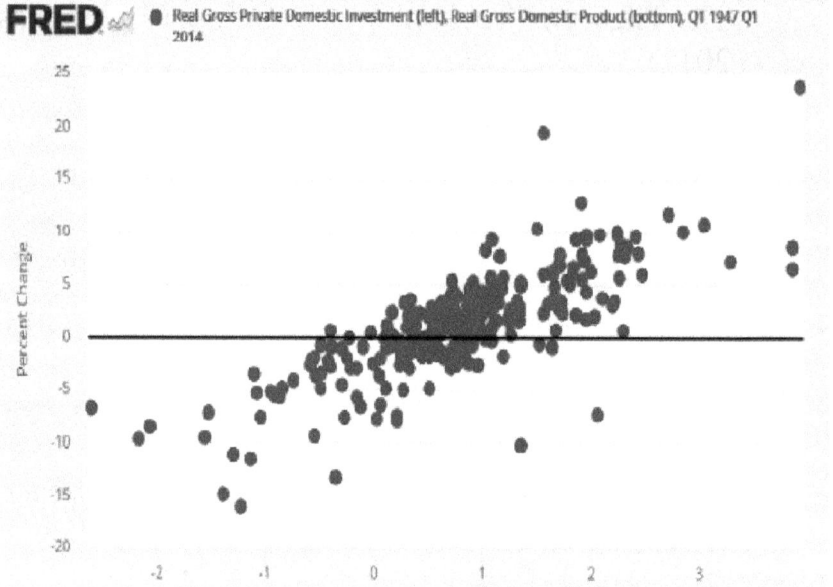

FRED ⦿ Real Gross Private Domestic Investment (left), Real Gross Domestic Product (bottom), Q1 1947/Q1 2014

The emerging national economic consensus that both Richard Florida and Brink Lindsey reference on innovation policy, would begin at the point where economists clearly identify the sovereign national economic interest of increasing the rate of private domestic capital to increase the rate of new venture creation in a decentralized metro regional policy approach.

Chapter 6. Envisioning A New American Knowledge Creation Innovation Economy.

Millennials are confronted with a political choice about the best economic system to promote fairness and social justice.

Currently, a majority of millennials support a type of crony EU socialism where fair outcomes are judged by a panel of political elites.

The argument made in this book for millennials is that this entire process of regional new venture creation generates a more fair income distribution than any other economic system currently available in the world.

In order to understand the flaws of the 3 current crony systems, it is best to begin by reviewing the difference between centralized economic information networks and decentralized economic networks.

All three of the crony systems feature centralized information flows and centralized control over economic decisions by the crony elites, who direct the financial benefits to themselves and their cronies.

Diagram 10. Comparing the Centralized Network to a Decentralized Network.

The New Networks

Centralized   **Decentralized**

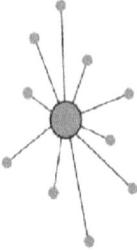

Centralized systems have a core authority that dictates the truth to the other participants in the network.

Only priveleged users or institutions can access the history of transactions or confirm new transactions.

Decentralized systems have no core authority to dictate the truth to other participants in the network.

Every participant in the network can access the history of transactions or confirm new transactions.

Credit: Ameer Rosic, BlockChain Geeks. https://blockgeeks.com/guides/what-is-blockchain-technology/

Millennials accurately perceive the unfair outcomes generated by the three crony systems, but they incorrectly embrace a diffuse, undefined socialist system, that they believe to be more fair.

Their embrace of the EU socialist system would succeed in replacing one form of American crony elite centralized decision making for another centralized system.

The better alternative economic system is the knowledge creation innovation economy where fair outcomes are governed by an individual's ability to appropriate the profits of their labor.

In the decentralized economic system, as currently exists in scattered metro regions, citizens are free to judge the truth content of a proposition to determine if the proposition is fair to their own financial success.

The decentralized decision making in the 15 biggest metro regions can be modeled as a block chain information network that aims at replicating the entire process of a regional private capital market, from idea generation to venture exit.

The intent and purpose of the block chain model of knowledge creation and diffusion is to increase the rate of new venture creation in the particular metro region.

The new venture creation process envisioned by the block chain model can be described as a series of "if-then" contingent statements, where any citizen in the region with an interest in economic growth could participate.

The series of "if-then" statements can be placed into a type of Bayesian prediction model that suggest that the prior industrial structure of the region acts as the foundation for future new venture creation:

- If exit events in the past create a pool of entrepreneurial profits, then if,
- The entrepreneurial profit is available to used to fund new ventures that create new products, then if,
- Technological genetic crossover within the industrial sectors of the region occurs between two products, then if,
- Consumers and markets select new products, then if,
- Complementary markets are created, then if,
- New patterns of income distribution are created, then if,
- New technological knowledge is created, then if,
- New technological knowledge is diffused, then if,
- New production assets are "called forth" from the expanding production possibilities frontier, the assets have a greater probability of being "inherited" by subsequent generations of products, and the evolution of the market can continue through a future attractor macro bifurcation and the emergence of an entirely new market.

A blockchain is, in the simplest of terms, a time-stamped series of immutable records of data that is managed by a cluster of computers not owned, or controlled, by a centralized organization.

Each of these blocks of data (i.e. block) is secured and bound to each other using cryptographic principles (i.e. chain).

Diagram 11. Regional Block Chain Private Capital New Venture Creation Model.

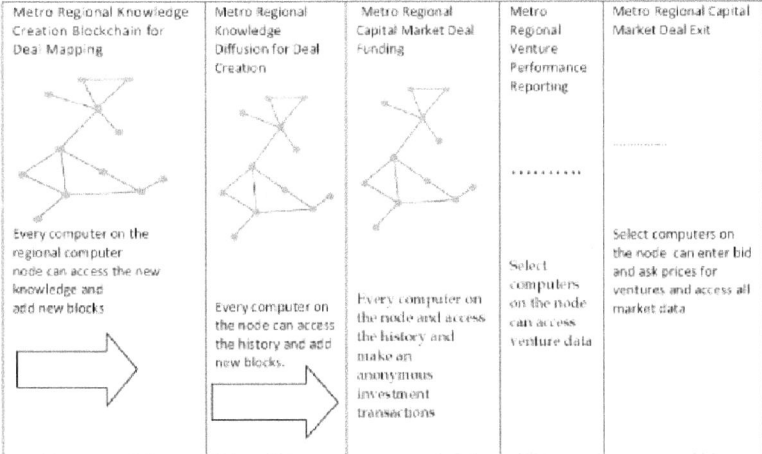

Metro Regional Knowledge Creation Blockchain for Deal Mapping	Metro Regional Knowledge Diffusion for Deal Creation	Metro Regional Capital Market Deal Funding	Metro Regional Venture Performance Reporting	Metro Regional Capital Market Deal Exit
Every computer on the regional computer node can access the new knowledge and add new blocks	Every computer on the node can access the history and add new blocks.	Every computer on the node and access the history and make an anonymous investment transactions	Select computers on the node can access venture data	Select computers on the node can enter bid and ask prices for ventures and access all market data

As described in Diagram 11, the entire process of new venture creation is envisioned to take place in a black chain network of computers, geographically located within 50 miles of the metro region.

The regional new venture creation blockchain is maintained by a peer-to-peer network. The network is a collection of nodes that are interconnected to one another. Nodes are individual computers that take in data, and perform functions that provide an output of modified data.

The "peer-to-peer network" partitions the entire regional economy to allow access by participants, who are all equally privileged, called "peers".

Computers on the node can add or modify data, with the ability to claim ownership of the new data. Each "block" in a blockchain contains specific information that cannot be altered, due to the distributed nature of the technology.

As a result, the blockchain technology has the potential to reduce uncertainty around ownership of new venture ideas and intellectual property rights and other property claims by providing verified records, and thereby strengthening private capital market institutions.

At the stage of raising private placement capital for a new venture, the likelihood of corruption, misunderstanding, and administrative errors is significantly reduced when a transparent, distributed, and immutable system is used to manage the transfer of assets from one party to another.

In the first block of regional idea creation, any computer member on the node can add ideas and comment on other ideas for new ventures. This block is envisioned as an open forum to generate ideas for ventures that may work in that regional economy.

This same type of information sharing currently occurs in the 15 U. S. entrepreneurial regions, described in Diagram 7. through business social networking events and angel capital forum.

Those type of forums would continue to exist, and be supplemented by the online block chain dialog. The first block in the block chain is the organizing tool to bring this set of potential entrepreneurs together to collaborate on new venture ideas.

As Saviotti notes,

> "...there is evidence from a number of studies to suggest that many of the important scientific ideas in the life of an innovation come from outside the innovating company, via these channels of professional scientific communication." (Rod Coombs, Paolo Saviotti, Vivian Walsh, Economics and Technological Change, Totowa, NJ: Rowman and Littlefield. 1987).

According to Rogers, in Diffusion of Innovations, the,

> "...communication channels, time and social structure are the key components in the diffusion process." (E. M. Rogers, "Diffusion of Innovations," cited in Rajeev K. Goel (Ed.), Economic Models of Technological Change: Theory and Application, Westport: Quorum Books, 1983).

The first block in the block chain facilitates communication among potential entrepreneurs who may not have previously known each other.

The communication in the first block supports and supplements the in-person, face-to-face networking events that currently occur in the entrepreneurial and angel capital forums.

Entrepreneurs come from the personnel ranks of existing production units. Entrepreneurs have been involved in a number of collaborative relationships with their peers about how things work, and how to make things work better.

The entrepreneurs are a part of a social-business network, whose participants communicate with each other to discuss and refine ideas.

Entrepreneurs leave the old production units to create new ventures, using the knowledge they gained about how things work, and with ideas about how to make the new venture more productive than the older units.

Ideas that gain community traction among participants in the first block are gated through to the second block for further processing into more definitive new venture ideas.

The communication in the second block brings in the set of professional advisors and other interested parties to view the progress of a potential new venture transaction.

In a process similar to current networking events, potential investors also have unlimited access to the shared data about a venture in the second block.

In the current model in the 15 metro regions, this process is commonly called "deal creation," where various legal and financial professionals collaborate with nascent entrepreneurs to refine the venture idea.

Any computer on the node can freely contribute ideas in the second block.

The nature of information flows changes in block 3 to be more like a member pass word access node of computers. The members of the node would be self-certified qualified private capital investors under the SEC rules for private investing.

The new venture team would prepare a private placement memo to place online in the third block, and conduct online forums for all interested investors, in order to present the venture concept and answer questions.

The capital funding for the new venture in block three would be in the form of bit coin or some other internet currency.

After the funding has taken place, only members who contributed private capital to the venture would be allowed access to on-going financial performance reporting on the progress of the ventures, in block four.

This periodic performance reporting would be somewhat like the 10-Q of listed public companies, but with less stringent auditing standards.

In the fifth, and final block, private investors could place bid and ask prices for the venture and transact secondary market exchanges.

If, and when, there was some type of exit event, the existing investors would be eligible to participate in the event.

The capital profits from the exit events continued to be deployed in new venture creation, creating a self-renewing, self-sustaining rate of economic growth.

In the case where there is no exit event, the investors can continue to monitor the performance of the venture, and continue to trade their ownership interests, in the closed, private stock exchange, much like they currently do in the pink sheets.

Missing from the block chain model is a necessary outside administrative institutional management component that guides the overall industrial technology innovation strategy of the region.

In the snapshot of the history of the regional industrial structure, the network of social relationships through which learning and diffusion takes place, is reflected by the presence or absence of technical coefficients in rows and columns of a regional econometric model.

In a type of Bayesian logic, the existing firms in the industrial structure of the region are the foundation for new venture ideas.

Based upon the structure of technology in the region, the econometric model could generate predictions about possible future economic scenarios

Morroni has described this existing set of firms in a region as,

> "...a constellation of firms with a leading firm and a cluster of complementary organizations, or a network of independent firms with collaborative relationships...these collaborative co-operative linkages enable certain economies of scale to be achieved through high overall production volumes." (Mario Morroni, Production Process, Technical Change, Cambridge University Press, 1992).

The matrix coefficients in the model represent a surrogate measure of the historical inter-industry social relationships based upon the assumption that if firms within a sector are buying and selling intermediate goods to each other, then they probably have engineers and technicians that are talking to each other.

This social business network of engineers and technicians are the people engaging each other in block one of the regional block chain to create and diffuse knowledge about potential new venture ideas.

The blockchain technology allows the entire process of regional new venture creation to be moved from physical interactions to internet collaboration.

The entrepreneurial culture of new venture creation would generate a more fair income distribution than any other economic system currently available in the world.

Chapter 7. Buchanan's Fair Constitutional Rules as the Foundation of the Entrepreneurial Economy.

Millennials consider the current income distribution unfair, but they make a mistake to assume that the crony capitalist system represents a free enterprise system.

The millennials embrace socialism because they desire that the unfair system be replaced by a better system.

The fair outcomes that millennials desire are obtained through fair constitutional rules, not by a panel of crony elites who judge the fairness of income distribution, after income has been earned.

In The Reason of Rules, (2000), Buchanan explains the importance of how citizens create fair constitutional rules when they provide prior consent to follow the rules that they give to themselves.

"Just conduct," writes Buchanan, "consists of behavior that does not violate rules to which one has given prior consent."

The issue of fair distribution of income and wealth can be resolved, according to Buchanan, when citizens are involved in the deliberations about creating the constitutional contract.

The differences in the level of citizen rule obedience between societies was explained by Buchanan in terms of the perceived "fairness" of the rules.

In Logical Foundations of Constitutional Liberty, (1999), Buchanan relies on a philosophy of logic to explain how the end goals of a constitution, clearly stated in the preamble, create the binding allegiance of citizens to follow the rule of law.

His first principle of logic is that all individuals are rational in the pursuit of their own sovereign life mission.

In The Theory of Public Choice, (1972), he defines an individual not so much from the perspective of insight-imagination, but from the brain's rational choice attribute.

Buchanan states that,

> "Uncertainty about just where one's own interest will lie in a sequence of plays or rounds will lead a rational person, from his own interest, to prefer rules and arrangements, or constitutions that will seem fair, no matter

what final positions he might occupy......we can simply define a person in terms of his set of preferences, his utility function. This function defines or describes a set of possible trade-offs among alternatives for potential choice."

Buchanan suggested that different constitutional rules produced different social welfare outcomes and income distributions.

Change the constitutional rules, suggests Buchanan and you change the distribution of income.

Buchanan's rules aim at creating a society based upon mutual reciprocity of fairness and trust.

The issue of trust involves the reliance of a citizen that another party to a financial exchange will reciprocate in the future on keeping promises that involve a future payment.

The issue raised by Buchanan, for millennials, is that it is impossible for millennials to rank the "best" economic system if everyone's preference rankings, in the initial creation of the rules, are not given the same weight.

In Buchanan's rules, there is no independent panel of elites who claim that they know better than the citizens themselves, what is in the best interests for society.

The main point of the Buchanan constitutional economic model is that the level of rule obedience depends on how the rules are interpreted by an individual citizen in affecting that citizen's life plans.

Voluntary allegiance to the rule of law, in the natural rights republic, results from the fact that all citizens have an equal opportunity for upward mobility and individual prosperity.

As Buchanan points out, voluntary allegiance to the rule of law results from the realization that it is in one's best interest for his or her life's mission to be consistent with the public purpose of the rule of law.

Buchanan argues that there is only one constitutional configuration that produces maximum economic growth, based upon maximum rates of knowledge creation and diffusion.

That constitutional configuration of rules creates the free enterprise innovation entrepreneurial economy.

That single constitutional configuration creates the maximum level of trust among citizens, so that citizens can trust each other to obey the rule of law.

Coincidentally, that same constitutional configuration also creates the maximum rates of knowledge creation and diffusion among citizens.

Maximum rates of knowledge creation create the social conditions for maximum rates of technology innovation.

Buchanan's rules link the individual choice, in the free market system, to individual choice in the political system because economic individualism is linked to equal political natural rights.

No other constitutional configuration starts out with this set of equal natural rights, aiming at the social goal to create "maximum" individual happiness. Equal natural rights create maximum economic growth, which, in turn, creates maximum social welfare.

The relationship between constitutional individual freedom and national economic growth is through the ability of individuals to create new technology ventures that commercialize new technology products.

Nations which have constitutional rules that aim at individual freedom and happiness have the greatest rates of economic growth and upward occupational mobility.

New future incomes, which are obtained if new markets emerge, and those new future markets have new products, that consumers favor over the old products.

New products and new markets may emerge, given a specific configuration of cultural values and laws that favor individual initiative and the appropriation of rewards based upon individual merit.

In The Lever of Riches: Technological Creativity and Economic Progress, (1990), Joel Mokyr reviews the relationship between economic development and technological innovation by first raising the question why economic growth occurs in some societies and not in others.

According to Mokyr, economic growth results from open flows of innovation, which only occur under one configuration of constitutional rules, advocated by Buchanan.

According to Mokyr, technological progress tends to occur in metro regional economies which have well-educated citizens, who are deeply engaged in the economic and political decisions of their communities.

In such a society, the appearance of technical progress is rapidly diffused, and as the knowledge embodied in the change spreads among citizens, it creates imbalances and bottlenecks in existing interindustry relations.

Economic growth caused by technical change is a result of capital investments made by entrepreneurs in new production units, that create new interindustry relationships and new market relationships that did not exist before.

The new ventures produce products whose supply varies, according to the feedback mechanism of consumer preferences.

There is no reason for millennials to try to "fix" the current constitution with socialism in order to obtain fair income distributions.

The current constitution is hopelessly flawed, and the political system has been captured by the crony capitalists.

In the current time period, there are no common values holding the citizens of this nation together in a common mission.

The current constitution finally evolved into a centralized, elite crony capitalism that is impossible to eradicate.

Attempting to replace the crony capitalist system with socialism, but keeping the existing constitution in place, would not solve the dysfunction in the American economy, or society.

EU crony socialism, and American crony capitalism are not based upon individualism, and those constitutional values are not comparable to the welfare outcomes of the individual choice model.

Generally, in the absence of fair constitutional rules that point to the goal of open competition for income, the reward structure associated collectivist rules about income distribution are manipulated to the benefit of the most powerful set of elites, who obtain power over setting the rules and the laws.

Unless the citizens agree, at the very beginning of the nation, of creating constitutional limits on the corruption of the elites, the national economy will not grow.

The economy will stagnate.

And citizens will end the economic race exactly where they started the race.

The current constitutional configuration inhibits individual freedoms and controls knowledge creation, in order for the elites to direct social welfare benefits to themselves.

Millennials should address their concerns about fairness and social justice to creating the constitutional configuration that creates the free enterprise entrepreneurial economy.

We conclude that young Americans have not been taught how to evaluate the differences between a collectivist economy and an individualist economy.

We agree with Clayton Christensen that there is a better, third way, than either crony socialism or crony capitalism. (Christensen, Clayton M. and Ojomo, Efosa and Gay, Gabrielle Daines and Auerswald, Philip Edgar, The Third Answer: How Market-Creating Innovation Drives Economic Growth and Development. December 28, 2018. Available at SSRN).

Christensen, et.al., state,

> "Market-creating innovations do exactly what the term implies: they create new markets. But these are not just any new markets; they are new markets that serve people for whom either no products existed or existing products were not accessible for a variety of reasons,

including cost or a lack of the expertise required to use them… the ideas (or recipes) that are critical to market-creating innovation, and that actually propel growth and development, are overwhelmingly uncodified, context dependent, and transferable only at significant cost—which is to say that tacit knowledge dominates, information asymmetries are the norm, and transaction costs are significant."

The tacit knowledge creation that he references occurs in business social networks among citizens who are deeply engaged in contributing prosperity to their community.

Christensen places the concept of innovation beyond the traditional economic interpretation as new product development.

Rather, Christensen sees innovation as a dynamic way of life that continually modifies market institutions by opening up new markets and new occupational opportunities.

He states,

"Innovation is the process by which institutions that are critical to development emerge. It is through innovations that create or connect to new markets that societies can create jobs, pay taxes, and, ultimately, build strong and lasting institutions... From an economic development standpoint, innovations can be market-creating or sustaining, or improve efficiency."

An innovative economy, in other words does not aim at maintaining the status quo of social class divisions and political power, as do the three crony economies.

Millennials who are attracted to fair outcomes of socialism would do better to promote Buchanan's constitution of equal natural rights at the creation of a new constitution, knowing full well that fairness in the outcomes of the innovative economy can lead to either success or failure, which is entirely dependent on one's own initiative, when the rules are fair to begin with.

www.ingramcontent.com/pod-product-compliance
Lightning Source LLC
Chambersburg PA
CBHW050737030426
42336CB00012B/1610